D1092698

DEVOTIONS
From The Earth
Kids Edition

·REPTILES & SMALL ANIMALS·

~~~~~~~~~~

Raise a child up the way
He should go, and when
He is old he will not
Depart from it

~~~~~~~~~~

~~~~~~~~~~

This book is dedicated to my
beautiful grandchildren:
Merrill, Tuck, Branch, Noah
Judson & Emberly

~~~~~~~~~~

Table of Contents

Chipmunks

...for every animal of the forest is mine...
Psalm 50:10 NIV

Chipmunks are one of the cutest small animals living in the forest. Their usual meal is nuts, seeds and berries. Sometimes they will eat the roots of plants in our yards, and then they can become a pest.

They like to gather and store food in their underground homes all summer long, so they have food for the winter months. They stuff their cheeks as they are out hunting, and then hide the food all over the

forest by digging holes to stash the food into.

There are 25 different species of chipmunk, and they all live in North America, except one that lives in Asia.

Chipmunks can be very friendly toward people, and we love to feed them in the parks and picnic areas. Some people have even had chipmunks as pets!

Chipmunks are also good for nature. When they eat fungi, they help increase water and nutrients for other plants. They also help plants grow by gathering and burying seeds.

What an amazing creation God made! Every little animal serves a purpose on the planet. People have a plan and a purpose too. We get to be God's ambassadors to the world. That means we share about God. One way we can share about our amazing God, is to talk about the creatures He made.

Research says that chipmunks only live 3 to 4 years in the wild. But when they live in a zoo, they can live up to 8 years because they are protected. In the wild, the fox, raccoons, snakes and hawks will hunt chipmunks for food.

Chipmunks line their underground homes with leaves, rocks, sticks, and other material, making them harder to see.

Prayer For Today: Thank you for the cute little chipmunk that is so friendly with people.

Chipmunk Fun Pages!

Help the chipmunk find the pinecone filled with pine seeds for its dinner.

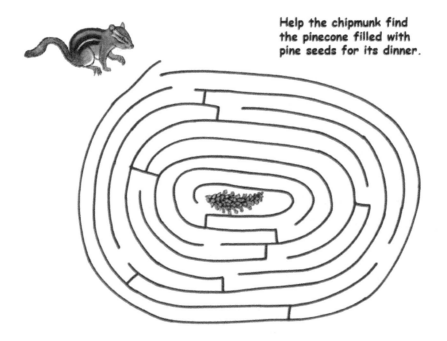

Toads

The frogs will leave you... Exodus 8:11 NIV

What's the difference between a frog and a toad? Well, toads have bumpier and drier skin, and are usually much larger than smooth skinned frogs.

Toads can puff up their skin to appear bigger to predators, and some toads have poisonous skin to protect them as well. **God seems to give animals all kinds of ways to protect themselves!**

New species of toads are still being discovered. One of the newest found species of toad is the 'Warm Valley' toad from Peru. The rusty orange coloring on these  toads make them hard to see among the dead leaves on the ground. These toads are so well camouflaged they are hard to find. That's probably why they hadn't been discovered until now.

The bible talks about a time when God sent an invasion of frogs into Egypt when Moses was asking the king (Pharaoh) to let the Israelite people go free from slavery. It was an epic invasion that changed the mind of the king. (Read about it in Exodus)

Did you know that today, we can still have frog invasions? A recent report shared about a new invasive species of frog on the island of Madagascar that is toxic  and killing off endangered lemurs that try to eat them.

Another invasion was reported in Greece in 2010, where they had to shut down a highway due a 'carpet of frogs' causing cars to skid off the road!

Prayer For Today: God your creatures are amazing. Thank you for sharing bible stories about how you've used frogs for your purposes.

Turtles

...all the creatures that move along the ground...
Genesis 1:26 NIV

Turtles are a very interesting reptile. Their hard shells give them protection because they can pull their head and legs inside the shell and wait for danger to pass. The shells will grow back and repair themself if they get cracked or damaged.

Turtles have a very special 'homing' instinct that allows them to find their way home even from an unfamiliar area. **Scientists can't explain how this works, it is just natural for turtles because that's the way God made them!**

Turtles like to live in grasslands, marshy meadows and in fields near the edge of a forest. They also are found near water.

Turtles like to eat plants, mushrooms, fruit, insects, fish, eggs and other things. They can eat a lot when they are growing, because they grow fast! When they are young, they hunt for food mostly near water sources. Then at 5 or 6 years old, they will start hunting for food on land and eat mostly plants.

Female turtles will nest during late Spring, and will lay 4 or 5 eggs that are round like ping pong balls, although sometimes they can lay up to 11 eggs! The mother will dig a hole to put the eggs in, then  cover the eggs with dirt. The eggs are then on their own to incubate and hatch.

Prayer for today: Thank you God for interesting reptiles that have special senses to find their way home!

Skunks

Every kind of creature that moves along the ground will come...
Genesis 6:20 NIV

It's common knowledge that skunks can be really stinky. **It's the way God gave them to protect themselves.** I mean, who wants to be sprayed by a stinky skunk, right?

When skunks feel threatened, they can spray their stink up to 10 feet away. The smell is very hard to get off too. It may take days or weeks of washing before you smell better! The best way to get rid of the smell is to wash with a mixture of baking soda and hydrogen peroxide.

Be very careful to keep a safe distance if you see a skunk, you don't want to get that spray in your eyes. It can cause you to be temporarily blinded. That's why skunks aim for the eyes of predators.

If you think about it, sin is like a bad smell on us that can only be washed away by coming to Jesus and asking Him to make us clean.

Did you know the skunk spray is flammable? It has to do with the chemicals in the spray.

Baby skunks can spray even before they can see, if they are In danger. Skunks only live about 5 years in the wild.

Skunks have homes underground called dens that are usually near streams of water. They sometimes take over dens that have been left by other animals. In the winter time, skunks don't hibernate, but they do sleep a lot more. Sometimes they can sleep for days during snow storms.

Prayer for today: Thank you God for washing us clean from all the bad smells (and sins) in the world.

Extraordinary Lizards

Small creatures and flying birds...
Psalm 148:10 NIV

The Blue Anole Lizard is unusual because of its color. They only live in one place in the world, on the island of Gorgona near Columbia. (Look that up on a map!) These lizards are very rare to find, and are endangered.

The Frilled Lizard is a rather scary looking creature when they puff out their neck frills to make them look really big to their enemies. They are found in Australia and New Guinea. (Can you find these countries on a map?)

The Monitor Lizard is a BIG reptile that is found mostly in Africa and Asia. They can grow up to 10 feet long! The Kimodo Dragon (one species of the monitor lizard) is the largest lizard in the world found only on the Indonesian Islands.

These lizards are very dangerous to animals and people. They have large claws and sharp teeth, and  their bite is poisonous like a snake. They have long split tongues like snakes too.

 One more extraordinary lizard is the Flying Lizard that lives in the rain forest of southeast Asia and southern India. (More map searching!) They don't actually fly, they jump and glide from tree to tree. These lizards will dig holes in the dirt to lay their eggs, but that is about the only time they leave the safety of the trees.

God has created many varieties of interesting lizards hasn't He? There are also many interesting varieties of people! Each one of us is unique and special.

Prayer for today: Thank you for so many interesting varieties of creatures and people.

Raccoons

..and the wild animals, each according to its kind.
Genesis 1:24 NIV

Raccoons are one of the few animals that have front paws that can handle things like human hands. It makes them so interesting to watch, but also makes them able to get into a lot of things they shouldn't.

They like to make homes in human areas like barns, old cars and other buildings, and they can be mean and dangerous if they find themselves cornered. So be very careful to keep your distance if you happen to find one living near you!

Raccoons like to sleep during the day and hunt for food at night. They like to eat fruits, berries, acorns and nuts. They will also eat frogs, fish, insects, mice and bird eggs. When food is scarce, you might find them rummaging through your trash cans, so beware!

Baby raccoons are called 'kits' or 'cubs'. They will live with the mother for a few months, and then start wandering away for longer & longer periods of time until they start living on their own at about 8 months old. Raccoons only live 2 to 3 years in the wild.

Raccoons are one of many interesting animals that God made. It's fun to learn about how they live.

Fun facts: Raccoons can run fast! Up to 15 miles per hour. Also, it's believed that the black mask around their eyes helps them see better at night by deflecting glare from lights.

Prayer For Today: Thank you for all the interesting small animals. I love to learn about your creation.

Prairie Dogs

...they shared everything they had.
Acts 4:32 NIV

The prairie dog is related to squirrels (without the big fluffy tail), and lives on the grasslands and prairies. You can see humps on the ground where their burrows are. They like to live together as families, and you'll often see whole

colonies of prairie dog towns with lots of piles of dirt. Some 'Dog Towns' can have hundreds of prairie dogs!

The bible shares a story about how **the first people who believed in Jesus lived together in communities** as well (See Acts). They shared everything they had with each other to take care of everyone's needs in the community. Today, believers gather in churches and still help each other. Prairie dogs live and work together like this too.

Prairie dogs are skilled fighters when they are attacked by predators and fight back with their sharp claws and teeth. They're cute, but you don't want to get too close to one! They can give you painful bites!

Researchers have learned that prairie dogs have a detailed language with each other. When they see a predator, they have a different sounding squeak or bark for each type of animal! They also like to greet each other with a nose nuzzle, which is another way they communicate with each other to say "hi".

Prairie dogs eat mainly grasses and leafy greens, but will also munch on bugs when they get a chance.

Prayer For Today: Thank you for the cute prairie dog, and the example in the Bible for how we can help each other.

Safe Snakes

...darting snakes. Isaiah 30:6 NIV

Snakes can be kind of scary looking, but there are really very few snakes that can hurt you. Let's look at some snakes that are safe to be around, and even to have as pets.

Corn Snakes are brightly colored with reddish orange and yellow skin. They are a popular pet because they are very relaxed and are easy to handle. They won't bite, and they are beautiful!

The Ball Python is another cuddly snake that makes a good pet, and they like to be held! They are also gentle and don't bite. They have black skin with golden yellow patterns.

Snakes have powerful muscles to move around without legs. They will sometimes coil up in a circle and 'jump' or dart to scare off predators or grab food.

The Rosey Boa is a common small snake that is easy to handle, found in the deserts of North America. These 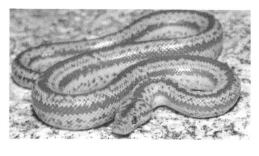 snakes have a light color skin with rose or salmon colored stripes that run down its back.

Snakes never eat plant matter, they always eat animals and bugs. It's interesting that some of God's creations in the animal world eat just plants, and some eat just animals, and some that will eat both! **Animals eat whatever God naturally made them to eat, but people get to choose.** He gave us all of it to enjoy! Some people choose to eat certain things, and it's all good.

One more friendly and safe snake is the California Kingsnake. They don't mind being handled, and some  even prefer it! They have black and tan skin.

Prayer For Today: Thank you for all the safe snakes we can have for pets.

Iguana Lizards

...lizards are unclean. Leviticus 11:30 NIV

Iguana lizards are one of the most popular reptile pets in the United States, even though they don't tend to live very long in captivity... usually less than a year. Many are turned loose or given to reptile rescue groups because they become hard to care for as pets.

These lizards are BIG, growing up to 6 1/2 feet long! Natively they live in the trees of Mexico, Brazil and central America. They like to eat leaves, flowers and fruit, and are excellent swimmers! If they are threatened in the trees, they will leap down to water and swim away.

God gave Iguanas a special super power! They can detach their tails if caught, and it will grow back without any damage. Most lizards have this special power. Wouldn't it be nice if we could grow back arms or legs!?

Iguana's come in different colors, but they all share the interesting back fin spikes and the beard skin under they chins. They also have razor sharp teeth and sharp tails to protect themselves.

Our scripture today says that lizards are unclean. This means we shouldn't eat them. That works for me! Would you want to eat that spiky guy?

Prayer For Today: Thank you for all the interesting reptiles to discover!

Foxes

Foxes have dens and birds have nests...
Matthew 8:20 NIV

The Red Fox is part of the "canine" family, and lives all over the world. They adapt to almost any kind of environment, including our own neighborhoods.

Foxes live in small groups, but hunt alone. They are said to be very smart animals. Sometimes they will hunt extra prey and bury it for later. They sleep during the day and hunt at night.

Most species of fox dig holes in the ground called "dens" to raise their babies, which are called "kits". When they aren't raising babies, they usually live out in the open, sleeping in little hiding places.

Fox dens are usually dug into the side of a hill or mountainside. They may dig two tunnels; a small one to hold food, and a larger one for babies to sleep in.

Other fox species include the grey fox, and the arctic fox. An interesting fact about the arctic fox, is that they shed their white fur after winter and grow black fur to stay camouflaged.

The grey fox has a little bit of red fur, but a black tipped tail. The red fox has mostly red fur, and always has a white tipped tail.

The Bible verse for today is Jesus telling his friends that foxes have dens to sleep in, but that he didn't have anywhere to lay his head. This means that during part of his time on Earth, he was homeless!

Prayer For Today: Thank you for teaching us that Jesus knew about foxes, and shared how he lived.

Horned Lizard

Let the land produce living creatures
Genesis 1:24 NIV

Have you ever seen a Horned Lizard? Unless you live in the desert, they are a rare sight. They are also called "Horned Toads", but look more like a strange lizard than a toad, with spikes on its back, horns on its head and a tail. They look sort of like a tiny dinosaur!

Horned lizards can hide in the sand by wiggling until they are all buried except for the head so they can watch for predators. They mainly eat ants and beetles, and the bugs walk right up to the lizard when it's hidden in the sand!

In the state of Texas, they call the Texas horned lizard the official state reptile, and they are listed as a threatened species, meaning they could soon be in danger of becoming extinct.

Some species of the horned lizard lay eggs, and other species have babies without eggs. There are many different types of horned lizards.

The short horned type have a very unusual talent as another way to protect themselves. They can blow

up their bodies to look almost twice as big as their normal size to look like a balloon! If this doesn't scare off their enemies, they have one more crazy thing to try… they can shoot blood out of their eyes! OK God, that's really creative!!

Isn't it interesting how some of **God's creations in the animal world are so similar, and yet so different?** Horned lizards come in different colors like yellowish, gray, or reddish brown, and they can have short or long horns.

That is very similar to the way God made people with different colored skin, shapes and sizes. Even though we may look different, we are all people made by God and precious to Him.

Prayer For Today: That you for so many different types of animals and people.

Lizard Fun Pages!

Start

Finish

House Cats

All kinds of animals... are being tamed and have
been tamed by mankind. James 3:7 NLT

Most families today have house pets, and today's Bible verse shows that this has been going on for thousands of years. **The Bible mentions birds and dogs as pets, and there is one story of a man who had a small lamb as a pet too.** Even though the Bible doesn't mention cats specifically, archeological evidence shows that there were cats living with families in bible times.

The records show that the cat was domesticated for living with people by the Egyptians many thousands of years ago. The Egyptians loved cats so much they made statues and worshiped them like little gods. We have even found caves with thousands of mummified cats, so they were very special animals indeed!

Today we love our house cats but we don't worship them! People have bred cats into many different species and it's interesting to see just how many different types of house cats there are.

The Bible tells us it's important to take care of our pets. Proverbs chapter 12 says, **"A righteous man cares for the needs of his animals."**

The most common house cat is the 'tabby' cat, which has grey and black stripes with white chests/paws. There are also orange tabby cats.

The 'siamese' cat has very distinct coloring, with dark colored paws, tail and face, with a creamy white/tan body fur, and beautiful blue eyes. This breed can have long or short hair.

Calico cats are interesting, because their fur looks like a lot of mixed cat furs! They are not a 'breed', but a result of random genetics that effect coloring. 99% of calico cats are female, and they cannot have kittens.

Prayer For Today: Thank you for all the pets we love, and for the beautiful house cat.

Porcupine

...as dangerous as a hedge of thorns. Micah 7:4 NLT

The Porcupine is a very interesting animal with spiky thorns in their back and tail (called quills) that make them dangerous to touch.

Porcupines use their quills to fight off predators. They shake their backs to make the quills rattle, and if that didn't scare off their enemy, they will run backwards into the animal attacking. The quills have barbs on them that make them stick in the animal and they release from the porcupine, but are hard to remove from the other animal.

Porcupines sleep during the day and are active at night, hunting for food. They eat tree wood, bark and stems. They can also eat nuts, seeds, grass and fruit.

Baby porcupines are called 'porcupettes', and a family of porcupines is called a 'prickle'. That makes sense since they are all prickly!

Mommy porcupines will take care of their babies for only a few months before they will be on their own. They are almost always born in April, May or June!

The Bible verse today talks about bad people who are as dangerous as a hedge of thorns, sort of like running into the back of a porcupine! But he goes on to say that **Godly people will look to the Lord for help from bad people. We can trust God to take care of us**. How does God help? We pray and he hears us. Prayer is just talking to God. When you find yourself in trouble with bad people, you should also find an adult to help as soon as possible!

Prayer For Today: Thank you for helping us when we need it. And thank you for making such strange and interesting animals!

Dinosaurs

Look at Behemoth, which I made... Job 40:15

The dinosaur is basically a giant reptile that lived before the big flood in Noah's days. All the dinosaurs were killed and buried in the ground by the flood, and are extinct now, but we do find their bones in the ground and can see what they might have looked like.

Dinosaur bones are found all over the world, and are on display in many museums of natural history.

Some of the dinosaur bones they found look like animals as small as chickens. Other bones were so huge, they estimate the dinosaur must have weighed about 80 tons!

So far, archeologists have discovered about 300 different 'types' of dinosaur bones. One interesting thing they have found in dinosaur bones is that they have a hole in the hip socket, which would allow dinosaurs to walk upright, which is different than reptiles we have today that crawl around on all four legs. That gives us an idea of how they roamed around the earth. They also found some bones that look like giant flying animals similar to

bats. There were also bones from animals they believed were ocean dwelling reptiles like giant swimming lizards.

Prayer For Today: Dinosaurs are amazing creatures. Thank you for the evidence that lets us discover these ancient extinct animals.

Rabbits

All the wild animals play nearby. Job 40:20 NLT

Everyone loves a fluffy bunny. The way they hop, hop, hop around is really cute with their big floppy ears and fluffy cottontails. There are 29 different species of rabbit, and they range from very small to extra large sizes.

Rabbits were originally from Europe and Africa, but today we find them all over the world.

Rabbits like to eat plants and grass mainly. But they also eat fruit, seeds, roots and tree bark. They usually hunt for food at dawn (the beginning of the day when the sun comes up) and dusk (the end of the day when the sun is going down).

Wild rabbits make their own homes by tunneling into the ground. These tunnels are called "warrens". Their tunnels usually have many entrances and exits so they can make a quick escape if they need it.

Rabbits have long legs and can run really fast, and for a long time, to escape a predator that might be chasing them.

Rabbits live in large groups called colonies, and will not do well by themselves as pets because they get lonely and depressed.

People get lonely by themselves too. **The Bible tells us to keep gathering together with other believers in church so we can make friends and encourage each other in our faith.** We all like to have fun with friends don't we?

Prayer For Today: Thank you for the furry rabbits that like to hang out together. Thank you for friends I can hang out with too!

Smallest Frogs

Moses cried out to the Lord about the frogs .
Exodus 8:12 NLT

The "little grass frog" in the picture above is the smallest frog in our country. They live in moist grassy areas along the eastern coast. Despite their small size, they can jump about 20 feet!

This "pumpkin toadlet" has been in an experiment that looks at the tiny frogs in the world. What they found out, is that these little guys  tend to lose their balance when jumping and can't land on their feet! What a crazy study!

Mexico is also studying tiny frogs, and found 6 new species that had not been identified before. This little guy, named the "cueyati"  frog is sitting on a Mexican coin.

 Here's another tiny frog found by researchers in the rain forests of Brazil. The tiny frogs are brightly colored as a warning to predators that they have poisonous skin.

Another interesting thing: tiny frogs have only two fingers and three toes because of their tiny size (rather than 3 fingers and 4 toes on normal size frogs).

God has certainly provided us so many things to research and discover! And we're not done. New species are being found all the time!

Prayer For Today: Thank you for all the tiny things to discover on planet Earth!

Alligators

In the end it bites like a snake... Proverbs 23:32 NLT

Alligators are one of the scariest looking reptiles in the world. They can get up to 16 feet long and up to 1,000 pounds. That's a big reptile!

Alligators like to live near fresh water, like swamps, marshes, rivers and lakes. They will dig in the mud to make a small home to hide in. Other animals like to use their burrows after they've left, so they help other animals in the environment that way.

When alligators are young, they eat bugs, snails and small fish. As adults, they will eat birds, turtles, snakes and small animals.

An interesting fact about these reptiles, is that they normally have about 80 teeth in their mouths. They frequently loose teeth, but can grow them back. So they might have as many as 2000 teeth in their lifetime!

Alligators are very good at hiding in plain sight. When they are just under the water with only their eyes sticking out, you can hardly notice them.

At one time alligators were becoming endangered because they were being hunted for their skins. People liked to make belts and boots out of Alligator skin. Since they have been given legal protection from being hunted, they are no longer on the endangered list.

When people work together to protect animals, we save them. **Our God wants to save all of us too, and he sent his son Jesus to save us for heaven.** Because we believe in Jesus, we can look forward to living with God in heaven forever.

Prayer For Today: Thank you for sending your son to save us for heaven.

Beavers

But ask the animals, and they will teach you...
Job 12:7 NIV

Beavers are amazing animals that are excellent swimmers and builders. They build dams in streams that become their homes and swimming ponds. Their big flat paddle tails help them swim and are used as a tool for building their homes as well. They use their sharp teeth to chew trees and make them fall down so they can be used as logs in the dams they make.

Beavers are vegetarians and eat only grass, clover, cattails and other bushes and weeds.

Animals make interesting homes in the wild don't they? **Did you know that God is making a special home for us right now?** The Bible tells us that God is making a new home for us, and Jesus called it "paradise". We can build beautiful homes here on Earth, but it will never compare to what God is preparing for us in heaven.

Prayer For Today: Thank you for giving us a beautiful new home to look forward to in heaven.

Common Lizards

...a lizard can be caught with the hand, yet it is found in kings' palaces. Proverbs 30:28 NIV

There are a lot of different common lizards that you may have seen around your own backyard. They live all over the world. They can live for 5 to 8 years in the wild, but much longer as a pet.

There are over 4,675 lizard species! Did you know that lizards smell with their tongues? And they have dry scaly skin that they shed as they grow bigger. One way they are able to escape from an enemy is by breaking off their tails. But don't worry. They can grow the tail back!

Lizards lay eggs but have to hide them real well, because other animals and birds love to eat the eggs as a snack.

A lot of lizards find hiding places under rocks or inside trees to hibernate over the cold months. Other lizards live in the desert and are fast runners over the sand. When it

gets too hot, they move under bushes or underground to keep cool.

Most lizards eat insects such as ants, beetles, grasshoppers, and flies.

Did you know there is a man in the Bible that ate nothing but locusts (a kind of grasshopper) with honey? His name was John the Baptist. He was the first person to baptize people, and even baptized Jesus. We still baptize people today to show that we are followers of Jesus.

The verse today says that lizards can be caught with the hand... have you ever tried to catch a lizard?

Prayer For Today: Thank you for all the interesting lizards in the world. And thank you for John the Baptist that taught us a way to show the world we follow Jesus.

Reptile Fun Pages!

```
A K H E Y O I T E C
Y L L E O G O P K R
Q R L T V R T O A O
B U P I T H K E N C
L S D O G C V B S O
G A I R E A X C S D
I S F G A X T I L I
E F W T T Z C O I L
E L T R U T I G R E
O R R N J U A L L Q
```

ALLIGATOR   **CROCODILE**   **GECKO**

LIZARD   **SNAKE**   **TORTOISE**

TURTLE

Voles, Moles and Gophers

The animals take cover, they remain in their dens.
Job 37:8 NIV

Voles, moles and Gophers are all known as pests. A pest is any animal that is troublesome to people because they dig up our yards and gardens, and make messes where we live.

Vole

These critters dig tunnels for homes which can kill anything growing in the area. This is ok in the wild, but not in our yards or gardens! Gophers and moles like to eat the roots of plants, and will sometimes pull the whole plant down into their tunnels to munch on. People start to see their garden plants disappear!

Mole

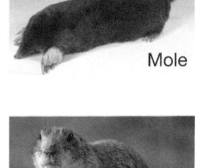
Gopher

Moles like to eat the worms and grubs in the dirt. All these pests can be hard to get rid of.

Did you know there is a verse in the Bible that says "I will prevent pests from devouring your crops..." (see Malachi 3:11) These kind of verses are called a "promise" of God. When we find a promise in the Bible, we can claim it for ourselves. This promise can be claimed IF we are faithful to follow God's instructions. Don't forget about the "if"s in the verses!

Now back to the gophers. They are famous for leaving dirt piles all over our yards. As they dig their tunnels, they push it out to the surface. What a mess they make!

These animals don't live very long - only 3 to 5 years, and can have litters of babies about 3 times a year. So they can multiply fast!

Prayer For Today: Help us to keep these pests out of our yards! And thank you for your promises in the Bible.

Chameleons

... the Chameleon. Leviticus 11:30 NIV

One of the most amazing reptiles in the world is the Chameleon. The first very interesting thing about these lizards, is that they can change their skin color to match their surroundings. This amazing ability makes them become almost invisible to predators.

Their hands and feet have thumbs like we do, so they can grip things as they climb that gives them special agility that other

reptiles don't have.

They also have very powerful tongues that can shoot way out of their mouths to catch bugs!

They also have eyes that can rotate individually, so they can see all around without moving their heads.

God has eyes that can see all around too. The Bible tells us that "The eyes of the Lord watch over those who do right.." (See Psalm 34:15 NLT) Isn't that nice to know? God watches over us all the time.

Prayer For Today: Thank you for the amazing Chameleon that seems to have magical color changing powers! And thank you for always watching over us.

Meerkat

.. every kind of clean animal. Genesis 7:2 NIV

The Meerkat is a cute animal that stands up on their hind legs and likes to hang out in big groups of their meerkat friends and family called "mobs".

Natively, meerkats live in the deserts and grasslands in southern Africa. They live in underground burrows that they all dig together with their sharp claws. Their burrows help to keep them cool from the desert heat, and usually have lots of tunnels and rooms.

Meerkats hunt for food during the day, and they like to eat bugs, small lizards, eggs, fruit and plants. When they have babies in the burrow, some of the meerkats will stay home to babysit, and they take turns watching the pups. They all work together and take care of each other.

The Bible tells us to work together and help each other too. "Each of us should please our neighbors for their good, and build him up In the Lord" (See Romans 15:2) Remember the golden rule: Do unto others as you would have them do unto you.

Here's an interesting fact about meerkats: they are immune to snake venom.

Prayer For Today: Thank you for the lessons to be learned from the meerkat. I will work harder at helping others in my family and my neighborhood.

Meerkat Fun Pages!

Copy the picture.

 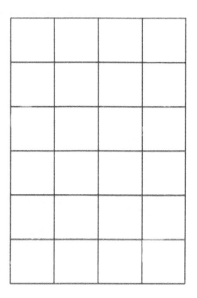

The Tortoise

...the creatures that move along the ground...
Genesis 1:26 NIV

Tortoises are giant turtles, and they live a long, long time; over 100 years. One tortoise in Australia named Harriet, lived to be 175 years old! It is thought that they have very good memories, and are pretty smart, even though they are very slow moving.

Did you know a group of tortoises is called a 'creep'? A creep of tortoises creeping along... that sounds sort of creepy, doesn't it?

Tortoises don't have teeth, but they chew with their sharp jaws. They like to eat grass, weeds, flowers and fruits.

Tortoises and turtles can stretch their necks way out to reach for tasty leaves, and can also tuck their long neck, head and legs into their shells to hide when it feels threatened.

We sometimes like to hide when we feel afraid too, don't we? It's good to know that God sees us, and is always ready to help us out of every scary situation. "I am with you, and I will watch over you wherever you go." (See Psalm 121:5) Whenever you feel afraid, thank Father God that he is watching over you.

Prayer For Today. Thank you for the amazing tortoise and for always watching over me.

Mice
Small creatures.. Psalm 148:10 NIV

A couple of mice make fun pets. The stores have cool mouse cages with toys and tunnels and spinning wheels, and the little critters love to run around and play with each other.

Have you heard of "Fancy Mouse Breeders"? They make a hobby of breeding mice with fancy fur colors. For example, look at these mice with spotted mixed colored furs! Some fancy breeds include long haired mice and striped fur mice.

Mice in nature (wild mice) are generally grey or brown in color to match their surroundings. It gives them a little camouflage for hiding from predators. They live in forests, grasslands and man made structures (like your house!). They typically dig tunnels underground to live in, and like to sleep during the day and hunt for food at night. They eat fruit, seeds and grains, but will eat almost anything.

Some mice have a very special purpose of being in scientific studies that help us in finding cures for sickness and disease. Being in research, and making us happy by being our pets are both special purposes for the small mouse.

God has given us a very special purpose too. We get to be his adopted children and share his love with the world.

Prayer For Today: Thank you for the cute mouse that gives us joy as pets, and helps us learn how to make cures for sickness and disease.

Dangerous Snakes

...venomous snakes...
Numbers 21:6 NLT

As you probably know, some snakes are very dangerous, because they can eject poison (also called venom) when they bite. People can die from these snake bites, so we have to be very careful around snakes.

The picture above is the King Cobra, a very venomous snake that lives in Southern Asia. The only place we will see these snakes in the United States, is in a zoo. Cobras are the only snake that build nests for their eggs.

The Copperhead snake is found in the eastern part of the USA. Their venom is not as poisonous as other snakes. It can make you sick, but won't kill you.

The deadly Boomslang snake is brightly colored and found only in Africa. They can have pink, yellow or green scales.

Diamondback rattlesnakes are common the desert areas and shake their rattles as a warning. If you hear a snake rattling it's tail, run the other way!

God made so many diverse reptiles and snakes!

Prayer For Today: Thank you that we can research and know about dangerous snakes. Help us to stay safe from harm.

Badgers

So the man gave names to all the.. wild animals
Genesis 2:20 NLT

God definitely got a little artistic when he made the Eurasian Badger, with their distinct black & white striped faces, they are hard to miss! These animals live in secret dens most of the time, only coming out at night to forage for food, so we hardly ever see them.

Badgers can smell things about 800 times better than we can. Maybe because of this, they are very clean animals, building bathrooms outside their dens, and changing their grassy bedding every day.

There are 11 species of badger in a variety of sizes and colors. The American badger is a golden brown color, with different stripes on their faces. American badgers will sometimes hunt with coyotes, and share their dens with other animals, so they are social animals.

Badgers use their strong digging ability with their long claws, to build elaborate homes underground with long

tunnels, lots of openings to get in and out, and places to sleep and store food.

God gives badgers special abilities, and each of us has special abilities as well. Some of us are good at building, or painting, or cooking! **God loves it when we use our God given special abilities to bless others.** Think about something you love to do, and that is likely the special ability God gave you!

Prayer for Today: Thank you for giving us each special abilities that we love to do and gives us a way to bless others.

Exotic Frogs

The Nile will teem with frogs. Exodus 8:3 NLT

Some very interesting frogs are called 'exotic' because they have uncommon features we don't normally see in a frog.

For example, the blue poison dart frog, which is only found in a certain area of northern Brazil. They are a beautiful blue color, but don't touch the skin - it's poisonous.

Then there's the red-eyed tree frog found in South America. The bright colors of this frog confuse predators so they can escape with big jumps into the trees with their sticky foot pads.

These cute little golden frogs have enough poison in their system to kill a human. These frogs live along the pacific coast of Columbia, South America.

Another interesting little frog, is the Amazon Milk Frog. The name comes from the milky white poison that comes from it's skin when the animal is stressed.

The Mimic Poison frog has the most interesting skin color patterns of them all. It looks like several different poisonous frogs, and that scares off its' predators.

God gave all these frogs special abilities to fight off enemies and survive in their little worlds. Frogs are important because they control the insect population and the disease that they can cause. **Everything works together in God's creation.**

Prayer For Today: What amazing frogs you created! Thank you for making life on planet Earth so interesting.

Gila monsters

...these are unclean for you: the weasel,
the rat, any kind of great lizard...
Leviticus 11:29 NIV

These rather large (about 2 feet long) lizards are dangerous because their bites are very poisonous. Twice as poisonous as a rattle snake bite.

The Gila monster lives in the desert, and eats eggs, birds, and small animals. They mainly live in underground tunnels and only come out at night when feeding, but they only feed about 5 to 8 times a year! So it's rare to see them outside of a zoo.

They move very slow, so they can't make a quick get away if a predator comes at them. Their only defense is their super strong bite and poisonous venom.

The Gila monster doesn't have very good eyesight, but they have a strong sense of smell. They will flick out their tongue to pick up  smells in the air like snakes do. They have to sneak up slowly on their prey, because they can't move fast.

When winter comes, they will eat before they go into their burrows to sleep for months. They store fat in their thick tails that feeds them during hibernation.

The Gila monster's name comes from where they were found; near the Gila River in Arizona.

Today's verse says that these big lizards are 'unclean' for us. This means we should never eat them. But really, who would want to eat one of these lizards for dinner?

Prayer For Today: Thank you for so many interesting creatures to discover, God!

Squirrels

God made the wild animals..
Genesis 1:25 NLT

Tree Squirrels are a very familiar small wild animal with long fluffy tails and grey, black or reddish fur. There are even white squirrels in certain regions.

They are amazing to watch scurrying up, down and around trees. Their claws seem to have a light but strong grip on the bark, and they have no problem running head first down a tall tree.

Sometimes you'll see them jumping from tree to tree across the branches high up in the trees, seemingly fearless about falling down.

Their favorite food is tree nuts and acorns. But they will eat almost any kind of seed, plus fruits and mushrooms too.

Squirrels are chatty little critters, barking, screaming and chattering to communicate with each other. They also will bark at birds and people who get too close to their nesting tree. You also  might see them stomping their feet and flicking their tails when they get perturbed!

Squirrels will bury some of their food for safe keeping, and come back to it later. But sometimes they forget where they've hidden some of the seeds, and they start growing in the spring! In this way, squirrels are like little gardeners of the forest. **God gave them a special task...these little guys help the forests keep growing.**

An interesting fact about squirrels: in Onley Illinois (where the white squirrels live), they have the 'right of way' in traffic, and you can get fined $500 for hitting one!

Prayer For Today: Thank you for the chatty little forest gardener, the squirrels, and how they help keep our forests growing.

Dogs
And God saw that it was good.
Genesis 1 NIV

It's a rare person that doesn't like dogs. They are said to be 'mans best friend', because as pets, they are so loyal to their owner and human family.

All dogs are descendants of the wolf. They have been bred into thousands of species, and have been domesticated into our favorite pet. Who can resist a little puppy?

There are 135 breeds of dogs today. They range from very small (1 1/2 pounds) to very large (200 pounds).

Dogs are very smart and can learn how to do things, respond to actions, and even 'speak' or bark on demand. Most dogs love to learn things because it means spending time with their owners playing. Other dogs are harder to train because they stress out under pressure. We need to be sensitive to how our dogs are handling training, and try to keep them happy. They are the happiest when they can hang out with us and play! Going for walks is a dog's favorite thing to do. They are so easy to please!

As a kid, having a dog can be a lot of responsibility. They have to be fed, exercised and cleaned up after. **God tells us that when we do good with one responsibility he's given us, he will give us more.** This is true for all responsibilities he gives us in life. It's how we learn skills for jobs and raising families of our own as we get older.

Prayer For Today: Thank you for how dogs love us so much, and for using them to teach us responsibilities that help us learn and grow.

Another book in this series: Bugs & Birds!
Available on Amazon or Barnes & Noble Online

Photo Credits:
Cover Photo: Chameleon, WorldAtlas.com
Chipmunk photos: havahart.com, facts.net,
Turtle photos: Smithsonian's zoo; Shutterstock
Skunk photos: Getty images; skunks.com
Blue lizard photo: Pintrest
Frilled lizard photo: biologydictionary.net
Monitor lizard photo: wildlifesos.org
Flying lizard photo: Draco Volans
Racoon photo: LiveScience
Raccoons running photo: Critter Care Wildlife Society
Toad photos: Shutterstock and Benjamin Marshall
Frog invasion: Pavlos Makridis
Prairie dog photos: worldwildlife.org
Corn snake photo: Kurit afshen
Ball Python photo: Krisda Ponchaipulltawee
Rosey Boa photo: Jason Mintzer
King snake photo: Robin Olimb
Green Iguana photo: Roy Toft
Orange Iguana photo: Robbie Labanowski
Fox photo: Animalfactsencyclopedio
Fox den photo: simplyappalachian
Horned Toad photo by KIKE CALVO and CosmosMagazine
Cat Statue photo from Wikipedia
Siamese cat photo from cozycatfurniture
Tabby cat photo from Carol M. Highsmith
Calico cat photo from lovetoknowpets
Porcupine photo: San Diego Zoo
Porcupine babies photo: Helene Cleland
Dinosaur bones photo: Natalia van D
Dinosaur art: Jerry LoFaro
Dinosaur illustration: Barbara Dziadosz
Rabbit photo by Octavian Cantilli, Omlet.com
Tiny Frog photo from NCwildlife.org
Orange frog photo from floridauseum.ufl.edu
Yellow frog photo from Christiansciencemonitor
Alligator photos from onekidnplanet.org, Skeeze/pixabay
Beaver photos: Chuck Caldwell, Robert McGouey
Lizard photos: Barry Yates, Iain H Leach
Mole and Vole photos from naturalgreenlawnandpest.com

Gopher photo by earth.com
Chameleon photos: IPfactly;
Meerkat photos: meerkatfacts; AZ Animals
Tortoise photo from OIST, scitechdaily, San Diego Union
Mice photos from vet voice, magnoliareporter, San Diego County News
Cobra snake photo by Parthkumar Bhatt
Copperhead snake photo: virginaherpetologicalsociety
Boomslang snake photo by William Warby
Badger photos from LiveScience, Tony Baggett,
American badger photo by Mark Newman
Red-eyed tree frog photo by Natallia Vintsik
Blue poison dart frog photo by AdstockRF
Golden poison frog photo by kikkerdirk/Fotolia
Gila monster photos by Krzysztof Wiktor, bepestfree.com, Will Burgess

Squirrel photos from pestworld.org, Picase, en.wikipedia.org
Puppy photo by -=RoBeE=-
Walking dog photo from lawscountrykennel.com

Made in the USA
Las Vegas, NV
10 April 2023

70419495R00046